CONTENTS

C000101650

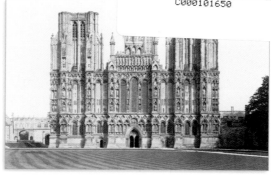

INTRODUCTION

Somerset is a county of great beauty and variety in its roughly 70 miles from east to west and 30 miles from north to south. Its northern boundary is the Bristol Channel, and in the south it comes to within seven miles of the English Channel. Sandwiched between the main body of England and the extremities of Devon and Cornwall, Somerset is a transition from the soft, mellow limestone hills that are such a feature of the heart of England to the wild, lonely moorland and rugged coasts that characterise the far west peninsula. Although not the largest of counties, it boasts a National Park in Exmoor and three designated Areas of Outstanding Beauty: the Mendip, Quantock and Blackdown Hills. Mention should also be made of Somerset's other distinctive feature, the Levels, vast tracts of land barely above sea level which are the finest lowland wetlands in Britain.

The north of the county is fringed with a magnificent sweep of coastline which runs from the Severn to Bridgwater Bay and Porlock in the west. It offers a wide variety of scenery. There are ancient ports like Watchet and Porlock, and wide estuaries with alabaster marbled ruddy cliffs and rocky headlands that make a wild contrast to the golden sands and pleasure beaches of Minehead and Clevedon. Flowing off the highest and wildest parts of Exmoor, fast-flowing rivers have gouged the rocks into gorges and hurtle down to the sea.

In the Middle Ages profits from Somerset's wool and cloth industries financed the raising of many elegant church towers in the Perpendicular style of architecture. The towers were built in several stages, each with pinnacles and buttresses, and the final stage included intricate tracery in the belfry lights. This became known as the Somerset style. The medieval wool wealth also financed the foundation of monasteries and abbeys. Glastonbury Abbey, with its early Christian traditions and dubious King Arthur connections, drew crowds of pilgrims, the medieval equivalent of tourists. In the late 18th century Richard 'Beau' Nash made Bath stylish for the wealthy and fashionable and the city is now regarded as one of the finest architectural achievements of its age. By the Victorian period the popularity of sea-water bathing led to the development of seaside resorts like Weston-super-Mare, Burnham-on-Sea and Minehead, aided by the arrival of the railways to bring in holidaymakers. Other visitors came to Somerset to thrill at Cheddar Gorge and explore the caves at Cheddar and Wookey Hole. These are all still major tourist draws of the county today.

Somerset is wonderfully varied in its geography, with wetlands, moors and hills, lakes and rivers, seaside and countryside. Its wildlife, plants and agriculture paint the land in a variety of colours and textures, each smudged like artist's chalk into the next, while the buildings are splashed with cream and honey – the colours of the stone sculpted from the limestone hills.

In recent years the historic county of Somerset has been reduced, with the creation of the two unitary authorities of Bath & North East Somerset and North Somerset. However, this book includes both these unitary authorities as it takes a brief tour around the traditional area of the ceremonial county of Somerset, with historical photographs from The Francis Frith Collection showing the people and places of Somerset in the past.

MARK, THE CHURCH 1890 23985

SOMERSET DIALECT WORDS AND PHRASES

'Addled' – gone off, rancid.

'Athirt' – across.

'Backalong' – some time ago.

'Bide' – stay.

'Cradlehood' – infancy.

'Crousty' – bad tempered.

'Dimpsey' – twilight, dusk.

'Muckers' – mates, friends.

'Right nottlin' – very cold.

'Ruckles' – peat stacks.

'Scrumping' – stealing apples.

'Scrumpy' – cider.

'Wha' be gwain 'ave?' – what are you going to have?

'Wha's 'ee to?' – where is he?

HAUNTED SOMERSET

At Taunton Castle it is said that the tramp of King James II's soldiers bringing the Duke of Monmouth's rebels to trial in the Great Hall can still be heard in the corridors, and a sighting of a bewigged figure in late 17th-century clothes, wearing long boots and gauntlets and with a pistol in his hand, has been reported on a landing. Sightings of a fair-haired young woman in 17th-century dress have also been reported in the Great Hall of the castle, and there have been poltergeist manifestations.

The pub and restaurant called The Friendly Spirit in Brook Street at Cannington, a short distance north-west of Bridgwater, was known variously as the Anchor, the Blue Anchor and the Old Anchor in the past. A pub since the 1760s, it was largely rebuilt in 1947 and was renamed 'The Friendly Spirit' in the 1980s on account of an inoffensive ghost that was said to appear in one of the upper rooms.

The Choughs Hotel in Chard is over 400 years old, and is said to be haunted by a number of unquiet spirits, including the shade of an old man who has been seen sitting by the fireplace in the bar and a mysterious shadowy figure that has been glimpsed around the building, but especially in the corridor behind the bar. Other phenonema include the sound of coughing when no one is there, and glasses being swept off tables by an unseen hand. A famous feature of the hotel is a mysterious tombstone built into the wall near the fireplace in the bar; it bears the weathered inscription of the name 'Winifred', but for some reason it was embedded into the wall upside down. A local legend linked with the tombstone is that no one has ever taken a successful 35mm photograph of it using flash photography, which is often interpreted as interference with the camera equipment by the spirits in the building.

SOMERSET MISCELLANY

The name of Somerset derives from the Old English 'Sumortunsaete', meaning 'the people living at or dependent upon Sumortun' – the small town of Somerton, north-west of Yeovil. Somerton was an important place in the past – from AD871 to 901 it may even have been the capital of the West Saxon kingdom of Wessex – and the 'Sumortunsaete' were the people of the area it controlled. The shortened form of 'Sumersaete' eventually became the name of the whole county, and Somerton was the county town in the 13th and 14th centuries. Inside Somerton's medieval church of St Michael and All Angels is a magnificent wooden roof with spectacular carvings. A famous decorative feature is a small barrel on the middle beam in the north side. Often described as a cider barrel representing Somerset's cider industry, this may actually be a punning reference to Richard Beere, Abbot of Glastonbury from 1493 to 1524, who probably commissioned the roof. The main features of the roof are the wyverns in the spaces between the king posts and the rafters – these dragon-like creatures with one set of legs and one set of wings were the symbol of the Anglo-Saxon kingdom of Wessex.

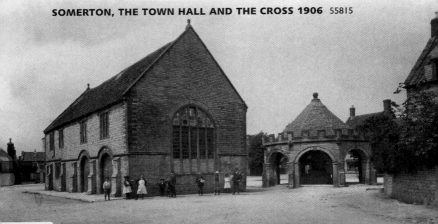

SOMERTON, THE TOWN HALL AND THE CROSS 1906 55815

A famous king of Wessex was King Alfred the Great, who ruled the West Saxons from AD871 until 899. In the early years of his reign he fought a long struggle against the Viking Danes who were overrunning his kingdom, and in the spring of AD878, on the brink of defeat, he retreated to a stronghold in the marshy area around Athelney in Somerset to regroup his forces. Later that year King Alfred summoned the people of Wessex still loyal to him to meet at 'the stone of Egbert in the eastern part of the wood called Selwood', near what is now Penselwood, north-east of Wincanton, for one last push against the Danes. A large force gathered to meet him, and King Alfred and his army marched to Wiltshire where they defeated the Danes in the Battle of Edington. The motto on the coat of arms of Somerset County Council is the Anglo-Saxon phrase 'Sumorsaete Ealle', meaning 'All the people of Somerset'. It is taken from the 'Anglo-Saxon Chronicle' for AD878 which records how in that year 'all the people of Somerset' rallied to King Alfred to help save Wessex from the Danish invaders.

The area of Somerset where King Alfred took refuge in the 9th century is part of Sedgemoor, a low-lying area that runs across the coastal plain and inland part of central Somerset from the edge of the Quantocks to the Mendips; it also includes the Somerset Levels, a vast tract of reclaimed marshland divided by the Polden Hills. Since medieval times the moors and marshes of this region have been drained by a maze of intersecting drainage ditches called rhines (pronounced 'reens'). The construction of mechanical pumping stations in the 19th century improved the drainage further, such as that at Westonzoyland near Bridgwater, which is now an industrial heritage museum dedicated to steam-powered machinery; with its 1861 steam engine and pump still in working order, this is the only surviving pumping station on the Somerset Levels with a still-functioning steam engine.

In the summer of 1685 many West Country people rose up in revolt in support of the Duke of Monmouth, the illegitimate son of King Charles II, in his attempt to oust his uncle, the unpopular King James II, from the throne. In June 1685 Monmouth returned from exile in Holland, landing at Lyme Regis on the Dorset coast. Thousands of people rallied to his cause but they were mainly countryfolk or small town artisans and tradesmen, and although Monmouth was proclaimed king in both Taunton and Bridgwater he failed to gain the all-important backing of the gentry. His forces were poorly armed, many with just farm tools, and were no match for the cannon and muskets of the king's army. Monmouth's 'Pitchfork Army' was eventually defeated on July 6th 1685 at the Battle of Sedgemoor, a few miles east of Bridgwater between Chedzoy and Westonzoyland, which was the last pitched battle fought on English soil. Over 1,000 rebels were killed on the battlefield and many more were captured to be tried by the notorious Judge Jeffreys at a series of 'Bloody Assizes' with what was seen even then as excessive severity. Hundreds of rebels were sentenced to death; they were hanged, drawn and quartered and their dismembered body parts were boiled in pitch and sent to towns and villages around the West Country for public display. Around 900 other rebels were sentenced to transportation to the West Indies to work for ten years in conditions of near-slavery on the sugar plantations of Barbados and Jamaica – 612 of them from Somerset.

The sad irony of the Monmouth Rebellion is that just three years later, in 1688, King James II was ousted from the throne in a political coup known as the Glorious Revolution because so little blood was spilt. He was replaced by his daughter Mary and her husband, William of Orange, as Queen Mary II and King William III. In 1690 they granted a free pardon to most of the rebels who had been transported to the West Indies. Unfortunately many of them could not afford the passage home, and their descendants still live on Barbados and Jamaica to this day.

There is a tradition in Bridgwater that the handed-down memories of local men transported to the West Indies after the Monmouth Rebellion who managed to return home was part of the reason why in 1785 Bridgwater became the first town in England to petition Parliament for the abolition of the African slave trade.

This 1930s view of the Cornhill in Bridgwater shows the statue of the town's most famous son, Admiral Robert Blake (1598-1657) in its original position in front of the Market Hall – it now stands at the top of Fore Street. Robert Blake became Bridgwater's MP in 1640 and fought for Parliament during the Civil War, successfully holding Taunton for Parliament against a prolonged Royalist siege in 1644-45. He was subsequently given command of the Navy by Oliver Cromwell, a position he held for nine years during the Commonwealth. His most famous naval victory was against a Spanish fleet at the Battle of Santa Cruz de Tenerife in 1657. His birthplace in Bridgwater now houses the Blake Museum, with collections of local and maritime history and particular features about the 17th century and the Monmouth Rebellion.

BRIDGWATER, CORNHILL 1936 87453

Set as it is in the Somerset Levels, the area around Glastonbury was marshy and prone to flooding until the development of modern drainage methods, and Glastonbury's famous Tor must often have appeared as an island in winter – hence its Celtic name of 'Ynys Witrin', meaning 'The Isle of Glass', referring to its reflection in the water surrounding it. In ancient times the Tor may have been encircled by a spiralling, processional way used by priests and priestesses to reach the summit for their rituals, and it must have had a strong mystical significance in the distant past – the famous landmark of the tower on its summit is all that remains of a medieval church dedicated to St Michael, the archangel who defeated the dragon, symbolic of the Devil, showing that Christians saw the Tor as a site of great pagan significance which needed the protection of their most powerful saint.

Glastonbury has long been associated with the legend of King Arthur, as the Isle of Avalon where the king went to die. In 1191 the Benedictine monks of Glastonbury's abbey claimed to have found a coffin in the grounds containing the skeletons of King Arthur and his queen, Guinevere, together with a lead cross with a Latin inscription identifying the man as 'the renowned King Arthur'. The remains were reburied before the High Altar but were lost in the 16th century. However, the whole story is now believed by modern scholars to have been a medieval hoax, probably to attract pilgrims to the abbey to help fund a rebuilding programme following a devastating fire of 1184.

GLASTONBURY, THE TOR c1965 G12078

GLASTONBURY, THE ABBOT'S KITCHEN 1890 23917

Tradition says that Glastonbury Abbey is built on the site of the earliest Christian sanctuary in Britain, and it was an important pilgrimage destination in the Middle Ages. Much of the life of medieval Glastonbury was tied to that pilgrim trade, and what is now called the George and Pilgrim's Hotel in the High Street was built in the 15th century to provide accommodation for them; it is a rare survival of a medieval pilgrim inn. The abbey was closed down by King Henry VIII in 1539 as part of his religious reformation and much of its stonework was robbed for re-use in the town, but the ruined remains are impressive and religious services are still held there regularly. The strange building seen in this view was the abbot's kitchen, dating from the 14th century, which is one of the best preserved medieval monastic kitchens in Europe. It was built well away from the main buildings to keep away smoke and cooking smells and reduce the risk of fire, and was designed so that smoke from the four cooking fires in each corner of the building would escape from the openings in the fluted tower at its apex.

CHEDDAR, SALLY SPENCER AND GLEN MIDDLE MILL 1908 60144

The Mendip Hills are the carboniferous limestone ridge that runs across Somerset between Weston-super-Mare and Frome. Underground caverns hollowed out by streams are a feature of this region, and the spectacular Cheddar Gorge in the Mendips is actually a huge underground cavern whose roof has collapsed. Cheddar is also famous for its show caves deep within the limestone crags, filled with colourful calcite formations of stalactites and stalagmites. The oldest complete human skeleton found in Britain was discovered in Gough's Cave at Cheddar in 1903, of a young man who died around 7150BC. In 1997 the DNA of 'Cheddar Man' was found to match that of several living descendants in the Cheddar area – there were direct matches to two local children and a partial match to an adult male who was, appropriately, a history teacher at a local school.

North of Cheddar is Burrington Combe, another limestone gorge in the Mendips, where in 1763 Augustus Montague Toplady (1740-78), the curate of nearby Blagdon, took shelter in a rocky cleft during a thunderstorm. This inspired him to write the hymn 'Rock of Ages' which begins: 'Rock of Ages, cleft for me, Let me hide myself in Thee'.

The Mendip Hills are veined with traces of 43 minerals including lead, which was mined from this part of Somerset from ancient times until the 20th century. A centre of the leadmining industry was Priddy, whose position at nearly 300 metres (1,000 feet) high on top of the Mendips makes it the highest village in Somerset. After their conquest of Britain in the first century AD the Romans were quick to exploit the mineral riches of this area and mined both lead and silver from the Mendips which they traded throughout their empire. 'Romans' were back in this part of Somerset during the Second World War of the 20th century, when there was an Italian prisoner of war camp at Penleigh, on the outskirts of Wells. The Italian POWS were put out to work on local farms and one of them was Gaetano Celestra, who had been a sculptor and mason before the war. When a stray enemy bomb fell at Beech Barrow and damaged a wall belonging to the farm where he was working, he rebuilt it and asked the farmer for permission to sculpt a she-wolf suckling two children, Romulus and Remus, the legendary founders of Rome who were brought up by a wolf, to place on the wall to remind him of home. The monument is beside the A39 road from Bath to Wells, on the left hand side as you approach the Mendip transmitter from the Bath direction.

WELLS, BEECH BARROW, THE ROMULUS AND REMUS MONUMENT 2004 W47726

At the southern end of the Mendip Hills is Wells, England's smallest city, which is famous for its glorious medieval cathedral. The cathedral is accessed from the market place through the 15th-century Penniless Porch, seen in the centre of this view behind the horse and cart; it was so-named because beggars used to shelter there and ask for alms from worshippers going into the cathedral.

The water streaming down either side of the High Street in Wells is not drainage water but a 'river' which rises from the springs behind the cathedral that gave the city its name; this is the only high street in England with a river running down it in this way. Along the north side of the street runs the gift of water made to the city in the 15th century by Bishop Bekynton through a conduit in the market place from the spring-fed lake in the garden of the Bishop's Palace. Much later, in 1803, Bishop Beadon provided a similar gift of water which ran down the south side of the street, for 'cleansing and fire-fighting'. Visitors are often puzzled to see the water bubbling up from the drains in the gutters instead of disappearing down them!

WELLS, THE MARKET PLACE 1890 23894

WELLS, THE CATHEDRAL, THE NAVE EAST 1890 23879

Wells Cathedral was begun in the 1180s and finished in the 1230s. Its magnificent West Front (seen on the Contents page of this book) is decorated with over 300 statues in its niches, which in medieval times were brightly painted. The statue of Christ in Glory presides at the top. Below this are the twelve apostles, then the nine orders of angels. The next row shows naked souls rising from the dead, and beneath this are bishops, kings, knights, saints, martyrs and virgins. Stone carvings on the lower part show scenes from the Bible; one is of Noah's Ark, and another alongside it shows Noah sawing up planks to construct the ark.

The beautiful scissor arches in the nave are the most striking aspect of the cathedral's interior. These inverted strainer arches were added between 1338 and 1348 as an innovative way of bracing and strengthening the central piers supporting the increased weight of the crossing tower after its height had been raised. Above the High Altar is the Great East or Golden Window with its magnificent medieval stained glass Tree of Jesse, one of the largest and most complete 14th-century windows in existence.

A few miles east of Wells is Shepton Mallet. A sight worth seeing in the town is the magnificent medieval wagon-roof of its beautiful parish church of St Peter and St Paul, described by Nikolaus Pevsner in the South and West Somerset volume of 'The Buildings of England' (1951–74) as 'the finest 15th century carved oak wagon-roof in England'. The roof is constructed in hand carved English oak with 350 panels, each of which is different from the others, and also features 36 carved angels along the sides.

East of Shepton Mallet is Frome, pronounced 'froom' like the river on which it lies. Frome was built on the woollen industry in the Middle Ages, when the river served prosperous wool and dying industries in the town. Like most of Somerset's former cloth towns, Frome's woollen trade declined after the industry moved to the new textile mills of Lancashire and Yorkshire during the Industrial Revolution, and other industries like printing and iron-founding took its place. The famous statue of Boadicea that stands on the Victoria Embankment near Westminster Bridge in London was cast at J W Singer & Sons' Art Metal Works in Frome in the 19th century, as well as many other well-known artworks around the county – these include the statue of Oliver Cromwell outside the House of Commons and the Statue of Justice that stands on the dome above the Central Criminal Court (popularly known as the Old Bailey) in London, and also the statue of King Alfred that stands in Winchester and is shown on page 7 of this book. The people of Frome took great pride in the statues cast in their town, and would often line the streets to cheer a finished statue on its way as it was transported from the Singer works to the railway station to be loaded onto a train and taken to its final destination.

The tiny car seen in the middle of the road in the photograph of Frome on the opposite page may be an Achilles, a shaft-drive voiturette that was produced in the town between 1903 and 1908 by B Thompson & Co (later Frome Selwood Motorworks) and marketed as 'the car for the man of moderate means'.

FROME, MARKET PLACE 1907 58843

Between Frome and Bath is Norton St Philip where the historic George Inn has had a continuous licence from 1397, making it one of the oldest inns in Britain. It was built in the late 14th century as a wool store for the Carthusian priory in nearby Hinton Charterhouse, with a secondary use as a guest house for the wool merchants who came to the town's fairs. On 12th June 1668 the famous diarist Samuel Pepys stopped at the George en route from Salisbury to Bath, and noted in his diary that he 'dined very well for 10s'. Pepys also recorded visiting the village church: 'At Philips-Norton I walked to the Church, and there saw …the tombstone whereon there were only two heads cut, which, the story goes, and credibly, were two sisters, called the Fair Maids of Foscott, that had two bodies upward and one belly, and there lie buried.' The Fair Maids were two conjoined twins who lived at Foxcote in the late Middle Ages, a small hamlet near Norton St Philip. The two carved portraits of their heads from their monument have now been mounted on the wall in a chamber under the church tower.

BATH, CAMDEN CRESCENT AND HEDGEMEAD PARK 1895 35749

Bath is famous for its elegant Georgian architecture and the hot sulphur springs that issue forth over a quarter of a million gallons of hot water every day. It was the Romans who first developed a health resort town there in the 1st century AD, building a sumptuous complex of hot spring-fed baths that can still be seen today. Bath reached its heyday as a successful inland spa and fashionable social centre in the 18th century under the reign of Richard 'Beau' Nash, the resort's Master of Ceremonies. It was rebuilt and greatly expanded during this period, creating a city that is one of the finest architectural achievements of its age, particularly famous for its magnificent crescents. As well as immersing themselves in the hot water baths of the resort, visitors who came to Bath for the good of their health also drank the rather foul-tasting sulphurous water of the hot springs – it contains many minerals and was considered a panacea for many complaints. The elegant Pump Room was built in the 1790s, where both the sick and the socialites would come to 'take the waters' and to see and be seen. Society people would engage 'aquatic doctors' to prescribe the proper dose of the mineral water for their afflictions, which is the origin of the slang word 'quack' for a doctor.

Bath Abbey was originally founded in the 7th century. In 1088 John of Tours was appointed Bishop of Wells; shortly afterwards he moved the cathedra of the Bishop of the Somerset See from Wells to Bath Abbey, thus becoming the first Bishop of Bath, and a large Norman church was built. However, later bishops preferred to live at Wells, which regained cathedral status jointly with Bath. By the late 15th century the Bath Abbey's church had become badly dilapidated. One night Oliver King, Bishop of Bath and Wells, had a dream in which he saw angels climbing up and down ladders to and from heaven, taking messages to God, whilst a voice called for a king to restore the church. Bishop King took the word 'king' to refer to himself, and he commissioned the leading court architects of the day, Robert and William Vertue, to design a new abbey church, the magnificent Perpendicular Gothic building that we see today. Its west front is famous for two ladders carved out of stone on each side of the west window, showing angels ascending and descending, commemorating Bishop King's dream.

BATH, THE ABBEY, WEST FRONT 1901 46462

North and north-east Somerset has mineral wealth in the form of coal, which was mined from at least the 15th century until 1973. The Somerset Coalfield stretched south from Bristol to the Mendip Hills, and from Bath in the east to Nailsea in the west. West of Bath in the northern part of the coalfield was the Pensford coal basin, with pits around Pensford, Hunstrete, Farmborough, Stanton Drew and Bishop Sutton; further south, most pits were concentrated around settlements in the Cam valley, such as Timsbury, Camerton and Midford, around Farrington Gurney, Radstock, Midsomer Norton and Writhlington, and further south again in the Nettlebridge valley, around Stratton-on-the-Fosse, Kilmersdon and Vobster.

As in all coal-mining areas, there were accidents and tragedies in the industry. One of them is commemorated at Midsomer Norton with a memorial in the graveyard of the Church of St John the Baptist to 12 miners who died at the Wells Way Colliery at nearby Westfield in 1839, when the rope on their cage snapped as they were about to descend into the mine. The older part of the memorial is a flat ledger slab that bears an inscription from the time of the tragedy recording that 'the rope was generally supposed to have been maliciously cut', although this was never proven and nobody was apprehended for the alleged crime.

The total tonnage of coal produced by the Somerset Coalfield reached a peak around 1901, when there were 79 separate collieries and production was 1,250,000 tons per annum. Several pits closed in the 19th century as the coal was worked out; those that survived until 1947 became part of the National Coal Board, but these eventually became uneconomical to run and the last pit of the Somerset Coalfield closed in 1973. Most of the coalfield area has now reverted back to rural countryside but there is still evidence of the mine workings and colliery buildings around the region, such as the fine red brick winding house at Pensford which has been converted into a handsome home. In many places you can also see the huge conical spoil heaps of the coal mines, known as 'batches', such as those at Paulton, Writhlington and the Old Mills batch that overlooks Midsomer Norton.

Opened in 1805, the Somersetshire Coal Canal was constructed to transport coal from the coalfield to its markets but its trade declined against competition from the railways and it had closed and been abandoned by 1904. Most of the canal is now filled in and lies derelict, but a short section has been restored at the Brassknocker Basin Canal Visitor Centre near Monkton Combe, 5 miles south-east of Bath just off the A36 at its junction with the B3108 to Bradford-on-Avon. The restored section of the canal is close to where it joined the Kennet & Avon Canal at the Dundas Aqueduct, just over the county boundary in Wiltshire near Limpley Stoke. The aqueduct is now the starting point of The Collier's Way (NCR24), a national cycle route that passes landmarks associated with the Somerset Coalfield and runs from there to Frome, via Radstock.

This photograph shows the Victoria Hall in Radstock, which was originally erected in the 1860s as a miners' recreation and reading room. Beyond the hall in this view is Ludlow's Colliery, which closed in 1954. Radstock's coal-mining past is commemorated with an old colliery sheave wheel that stands in front of the town's museum, a fascinating place to visit for anyone interested in the industrial and social heritage of the communities of the Somerset Coalfield.

RADSTOCK, VICTORIA HALL c1950 R2003

It was the existence of coal mines around Nailsea in North Somerset that attracted the glass manufacturer John Robert Lucas to establish his glassworks there in 1788, triggering an important glass industry in the town. The plentiful coal supplies fuelled the furnace cones where the glass was produced. At that time there was a heavy tax on the clearest and most brilliant grades of glass used to make high quality items such as tableware, but a lower tax on the lower grade glass used to make bottle glass or window glass – known as 'crown glass – and it was this type that was made at Nailsea. However, the glassworkers often used up any leftover residue of glass at the end of their shifts to make a wide range of fancy goods that they decorated very simply. These included jugs, bottles, flasks, mugs, tankards, bowls, vases, jars, rolling pins, paperweights, pipes and walking sticks. Although these items were made from lower grade glass they were of such high quality that they became very popular, and 'Nailsea' glassware is still sought after by collectors around the world. The Nailsea glassworks closed down in the 1870s after coal supplies began to dwindle, but the industry is recalled in the name of the Crown Glass Shopping Centre in the town, and a statue of a glassworker stands near the site of the glassworks beside the road outside the Tesco supermarket, at the junction of High Street with Brockway.

North of Nailsea and around the coastal towns of Portishead and Clevedon on the Severn Estuary are a number of places with 'in-Gordano' in their placenames – Easton-in-Gordano, Clapton-in-Gordano, Weston-in-Gordano and Walton-in-Gordano. The 'Gordano' part of the names is a Latinised form of the Old English word 'Gorden' which means 'muddy valley'; this is a reference to the valley area that roughly forms a triangular shape from points between Easton-in-Gordano, Portishead and Clevedon and is a region of low-lying reclaimed marshy land just above sea level.

Clevedon's pier was described as 'the most beautiful pier in England' by Sir John Betjeman, founder of The National Piers Society. The pier was first opened in 1869, having been built using rails from the defunct South-West Railway. This photograph shows it before the original wooden pierhead was replaced by a cast-iron structure in 1893, and an ornate pavilion was added the following year. The pier's construction is light and graceful, looking far too delicate to survive the storms that periodically batter the coast, and two spans collapsed in 1970. Its future seemed very doubtful but the pier survived a public enquiry about its possible demolition in 1980, with the Environment Secretary calling it an 'exceptionally important building'. Many years of dedicated work then took place to restore the pier and it was reopened to the public in its entirety in 1998. In 2001 the pier was upgraded to a Grade 1 listed building – the only other pier with this status is Brighton's West Pier, but that structure is currently derelict after being damaged by storms and fire between 2002 and 2004, so Clevedon Pier is the only remaining intact Grade 1 listed pier in the country.

CLEVEDON, THE PIER 1892 31251

Portishead and Clevedon lie beside the waters of the Severn Estuary, and the Bristol Channel properly begins at Weston-super-Mare – the lower limit of the Severn Estuary and the start of the Bristol Channel is marked by Sand Point, just to the north of the town.

'I'm off to sunny Weston-super-Mare, They say you'll always find a welcome way down there' sang The Wurzels, North Somerset's first supergroup (famous for such classics as 'Drink Up Thy Zider', 'I've Got a Brand New Combine Harvester' and 'When the Common Market Comes to Stanton Drew'), and Weston has been welcoming visitors since it first developed from a fishing village into a seaside pleasure ground in the early 19th century. However, this point of the Bristol Channel has the second highest tidal range in the world, and when day trippers arrived at Weston during low tide in the past, when it seemed as if the sea had ebbed away to America, they were often disappointed at not being able to have a dip or a paddle. The problem was solved in the 1920s when unemployed Welsh miners were drafted into Weston on a job creation scheme to build a causeway linking Knightstone Island and Claremont which created Marine Lake, a permanent enclosed high water bathing place where visitors can swim and paddle whatever the state of the tides.

South-west of Weston-super-Mare across the estuary of the River Axe is the high promontory of Brean Down. This was used as a test launch site for rockets and experimental weapons during the Second World War, and the large concrete arrow that was constructed on the down to direct bombers to the practice range can still be seen.

WESTON-SUPER-MARE, THE PARADE
1901 47874

Pisa in Italy is famous for its leaning tower, but Burnham-on-Sea in Somerset has one too! The 14th-century St Andrew's Church that stands on the seafront was built on poor foundations and its tower now leans almost 92 cms (3 feet) out of the vertical. Inside the church are sculptures from a reredos, or altar piece, that was commissioned by King James II in 1686 for the chapel of Whitehall Palace. It was designed by Inigo Jones and carved in marble by Grinling Gibbons. After a chequered history, in 1820 the reredos was given by King George IV to the Bishop of Rochester; he was also the Vicar of Burnham, and he had it brought to the town to decorate the church. A subsequent vicar had the reredos dismantled and thrown out, but some parts were later salvaged and restored to the church and are now dispersed around the interior, including behind the altar.

A landscape feature of this part of Somerset is Brent Knoll, a few miles east of Burnham-on-Sea. Legend credits its creation to the Devil who flung a spadeful of earth that fell short of the sea when he was excavating Cheddar Gorge. This isolated Blue Lias limestone outlier rises steeply from the flat land surrounding it and is topped by one of Somerset's finest Iron Age hill forts. The knoll gives its name to the nearby village of Brent Knoll, whose parish church of St Michael is famous for its medieval woodwork, particularly an extraordinary series of three carved wooden bench ends depicting the savage punishment meted out by a group of birds to a fox dressed in the robes and mitre of an abbot. This is an early example of political satire which is often interpreted as a lampoon of the villagers' displeasure with an avaricious Abbot of Glastonbury following some sort of disagreement over rents or revenues, with the fox representing the abbot and the birds representing the villagers themselves; however, an alternative theory is that the fox represents the unpopular Richard Foxe, Bishop of Bath and Wells, who took up office in 1492.

Our tour now moves into West Somerset and the beautiful Quantock Hills, the first Area of Outstanding Natural Beauty created in the UK. In 1797 the Romantic poet Samuel Taylor Coleridge (1772-1834) and his wife and baby son came to live in the Quantocks, at what is now called Coleridge Cottage in Lime Street in Nether Stowey, which was their home for the next three years.

Coleridge wrote his best poems during this time in his 'Beloved Stowey', including 'Frost at Midnight', 'The Nightingale', and 'This Lime Tree Bower, My Prison'. Coleridge was visited at Nether Stowey by his friend and fellow poet William Wordsworth, who was so enchanted by the area that he rented Alfoxton House at nearby Holford and lived there for a year with his sister Dorothy. The three friends loved to take long walks around the area ('Upon smooth Quantock's airy ridge we roved') and during this time Coleridge and Wordsworth wrote the collection of poems they published as 'Lyrical Ballads' in 1798; this included Coleridge's famous work 'The Rime of the Ancient Mariner', which was inspired by a neighbour's nightmare about a spectral ship. Dorothy Wordsworth recorded in her journal how on one of their walking tours they went to Watchet on the West Somerset coast and Coleridge imagined the mariner of his poem setting out from its ancient harbour, later returning there to tell his woeful tale: 'Here', he told Wordsworth, 'is where he shall set out on his fateful voyage.' A dramatic modern statue of the Ancient Mariner now stands beside Watchet's harbour, complete with the albatross that he foolishly killed; by doing this he aroused the wrath of the sea-spirits and doomed himself and the crew of his ship to a terrible fate.

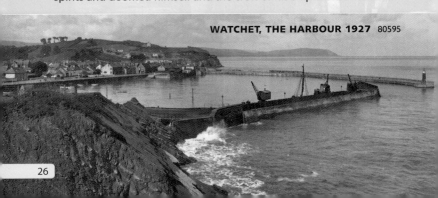

WATCHET, THE HARBOUR 1927 80595

A few miles inland from Watchet near the village of Washford are the impressive and atmospheric ruins of Cleeve Abbey, now in the care of English Heritage. Although nothing can be seen now of the abbey church except its excavated foundations, the rest of the monastic buildings are in an excellent state because after the abbey's dissolution in the 16th century they were used as farm buildings until the late 19th century and kept intact. Cleeve Abbey is one of the few 13th-century monastic sites where you can see such a complete set of buildings, including the monks' living quarters, and it is relatively easy for the visitor to grasp the typical layout of a Cistercian abbey and to imagine what the daily life of a monk might be like. Interesting features of the ruins are the ornate timber roof of the refectory, supported by carved angel corbels, the wall painting of the painted chamber and a rare Collation Seat, a shallow, trefoil-headed recess in the north wall of the cloister which framed the abbot's chair when he sat there for the Collation ceremony, the spiritual readings that took place every evening for which the monastic community gathered after Vespers and before the last service of the day, Compline.

Further west along the A39 from Washford towards Minehead is Carhampton, where the Butchers Arms pub has a date of 1638 in sheep's knucklebones set into the floor of the bar, recording when the building first became an inn, or more probably a cider house. The Butchers Arms is one of the few pubs in the country that still continues the ancient tradition of a wassailing ceremony, which is held in the orchard behind the building every January 17th, 'Old Twelfth Night' according to the old-style Julian Calendar, to scare away evil spirits from the apple trees for a good harvest the following year. Villagers gather in the orchard and form a circle around the largest apple tree, where they pour cider on the roots of the tree and hang pieces of toast soaked in cider in the branches for the robins, who represent the 'good spirits' of the tree. A shotgun is then fired overhead to scare away evil spirits, and the traditional Carhampton Wassailing Song is sung.

DUNSTER, THE LUTTRELL ARMS, MARKET HOUSE AND CASTLE c1880 15837

Every Christmas Eve a custom called 'Burning the Ashen Faggot' takes place in the Luttrell Arms at Dunster, a few miles south-east of Minehead. In this very old Christmas tradition, originating from a legend that the Christ-child was first warmed by a fire of green ash, twelve thick sticks are bound up in a bundle, the 'faggot', tied with green ash bands. The faggot is then burned in the huge fireplace of the hotel whilst the Dunster Carol is sung, and a round of drinks is ordered when each binding burns and bursts. A more recent winter tradition in the village is Dunster by Candlelight, which began in 1987 and takes place on the first Friday and Saturday in December, when the village gives up electricity and lights its streets with candles and lanterns. The event begins with the Lantern Lighting Procession on the Friday night, when the village children and their families accompany tall stilt walkers in colourful costumes along the streets as they put up the lanterns. The event also features a variety of street entertainment on both nights, including carol singers, Morris dancers, fairground organs, handbell-ringing and choral singing in the parish church.

Minehead is famous for its ancient and colourful Hobby Horse tradition linked with May Day – the 1st of May. There are actually three Hobby Horses, the Original Sailor's Horse and its more recent rivals, the Traditional Sailor's Horse and the Town Horse. Each horse is made of a boat-shaped wooden frame covered with painted fabric and ribbons, below which is a long fabric skirt decorated with brightly painted roundels. The frame is carried on the shoulders of a dancer concealed inside, wearing a long pointed hat with his face concealed by a mask. They make their first appearance on May Day Eve each year and then prance their way around the town and the surrounding area for the next three days, performing a variety of antics and chasing the children that follow them, all the while accompanied by drummers, musicians and 'gullivers' – dancers masked and dressed similarly to the horses, but without the wooden frame. The Hobby Horses supposedly leave good luck behind them, and donations collected from the crowd watching them are given to local charities. There are several theories about the origins of the Hobby Horse custom: one is that it dates back to the 9th century and commemorates when a Minehead crew disguised their ship as a sea serpent and frightened away Viking raiders, whilst another is that the Hobby Horse represents the King of the May and the custom is a survival of ancient fertility rites celebrating the coming of spring. The latter is given credence by the local legend that if a young woman is lashed by the long tail attached to the end of the horse she will give birth to twins.

MINEHEAD, THE BEACH 1906 57157

Did You Know?

SOMERSET

A MISCELLANY

Moving west from Minehead the A39 reaches the charming village of Porlock, a mile inland from the coast, where the lanes and streets wind delightfully between attractive whitewashed and thatched houses. At one time the sea extended to Porlock itself, but a retreating shoreline over the centuries has left it over a mile inland and the harbour is now at Porlock Weir, which was named from the old fish weir or trap on the beach. The parish church of Porlock is dedicated to the 6th-century Welsh Celtic saint Dubricius and has a 13th-century tower with a later shingled spire which is curiously truncated. There is a local legend that the top of its spire was cut off in the early 19th century and taken to adorn the small church at Culbone, a short distance further west along the coast, where the short shingled spire rising from the nave roof forms an unusual feature of the church – as seen in the photograph on the opposite page.

PORLOCK, THE CHURCH 1907 58348

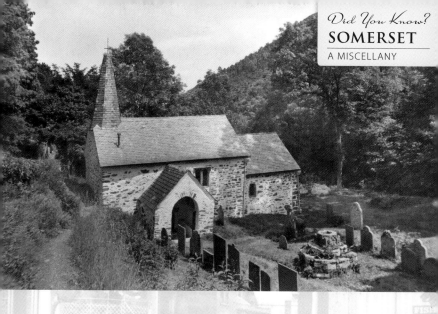

CULBONE, THE SMALLEST PARISH CHURCH IN ENGLAND 1929
82194

Culbone's tiny church of St Beuno is sited near the Somerset coast in a steep wooded combe that runs to the sea. The remote church is well-known to walkers along the South West Coast Path but is inaccessible by public road, and is reached by a footpath through the woods that surround it. Partly Norman, at just 35 feet long by 12 feet 4 inches wide it is reputed to be the smallest complete parish church in England still in regular use despite the lack of road access – many other 'smallest churches' in the country are actually only surviving parts of what were originally much larger churches. In the 16th and early 17th centuries the woods around the church were home to a colony of lepers and in the north wall of the church is a narrow window, known as a leper's squint, through which those suffering from this dreadful disease could follow the church services from outside the building.

EXMOOR, DUNKERY BEACON 1921 75007

The jewel in West Somerset's crown is Exmoor, a wild place of high, rounded hills and colourful heaths, bright with purple heather and yellow gorse. Its highest point is Dunkery Beacon on the summit of Dunkery Hill, 4 miles south of Porlock. The moorland is roamed by sheep, the largest number of wild red deer outside Scotland and semi-wild Exmoor Ponies – although they live rough on the moor all year round, they all belong to somebody. The Exmoor Pony is distinguished by its russet brown colouring with shading of a paler light fawn colour, known as 'mealy', around the eyes, muzzle, flanks and underbelly. It is Britain's oldest native equine breed and very hardy, but its numbers have declined in recent years and it has been given 'endangered' status by the Rare Breeds Survival Trust. In 2000 the Moorland Mousie Trust was established to promote and conserve the Exmoor Pony; based at The Exmoor Pony Centre at Ashwick, near Dulverton, the trust is doing sterling work to ensure this breed does not become extinct. You can get involved by adopting an Exmoor Pony to help fund their work – see their website: www.moorlandmousietrust.org.uk.

In the extreme north-western corner of Exmoor is the small village of Oare. From 1809 until 1842 the rector of St Mary's Church in Oare was John Blackmore. His grandson Richard Doddridge Blackmore (1825-1900) regularly visited him there as a child and got to know the area well. Later in his life he recorded his childhood memories: 'Sometimes of a night, when the spirit of a dream flits away…I behold an old man, with a keen profile under a parson's shovel hat, riding a tall chestnut horse up the western slope of Exmoor, followed by his little grandson upon a shaggy pony'. In later years R D Blackmore immortalised this part of Exmoor in his classic novel 'Lorna Doone'. The tale is set at the time of the Monmouth Rebellion in the 1680s and is woven around both fact and fiction. It is based on stories of the Doone, or Doune, gang, a family of Scottish outlaws who arrived on Exmoor in the early 17th century and settled in a remote combe in the Badgworthy Water region on the boundary of Somerset and Devon, from where they terrorised the local people with acts of robbery, extortion and murder. R D Blackmore featured many real places in his book, and it was at his grandfather's church at Oare that he set the dramatic scene of the marriage of Lorna to her sweetheart John Ridd, where she was shot at the altar by a musket ball fired through a church window by the evil villain, Carver Doone, just after taking her wedding vows.

OARE, THE VALE AND ST MARY'S CHURCH c1960
O3003

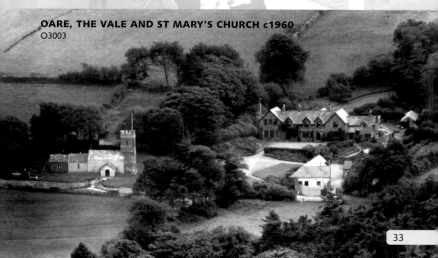

Wheddon Cross stands at a crossroads of the A396 with the B3224 on the ridge between Exmoor and the Brendon Hills, where in the past the long haul up the turnpike road from Bampton or Minehead gave the Rest and Be Thankful Inn in the village its well-earned name. A famous feature near Wheddon Cross is Snowdrop Valley, which is carpeted with a spectacular blanket of snowdrops in February. This hidden valley along the River Avill is privately owned, but is opened to the public for a few weeks every spring to allow people to enjoy Nature's display. See the Wheddon Cross village website for information about opening times and how to get there: www.wheddoncross.org.uk.

South of Wheddon Cross is Winsford, seen in this view nestling in the upper valley of the River Exe, with the valley of the Winn Brook winding up to the left. The watercourses that flow through Winsford are crossed by eight tiny stone bridges, adding to the charm of this picturesque village. In the foreground of this view are Closewool sheep, a hardy breed typical of Exmoor that is well suited to the extreme weather conditions of this exposed upland region.

WINSFORD, GENERAL VIEW c1960 W112018

EXMOOR, TARR STEPS 1929 82159a

A few miles south-west of Winsford is one of Exmoor's most famous landmarks, the ancient clapper bridge made of flat stone slabs known as Tarr Steps across the River Barle. The entire structure is 55 metres (180ft) long with 17 spans, or arches, and nothing but the weight of the stone holds them in place. According to a local legend, the bridge was set in place by the Devil and although he was successfully challenged by a local parson to allow people to use the bridge to cross the river, he still retains sunbathing rights on the stones! The Barle can flood violently, and the bridge has been washed away several times within living memory. The slabs are now numbered so they can be retrieved and replaced in the correct order whenever this happens again.

TAUNTON, FORE STREET 1925 78807

Our tour now moves to Taunton, Somerset's county town. Taunton has a castle that witnessed sieges and battles during the Wars of the Roses and the Civil War and the Bloody Assizes of Judge Jeffreys; the inner ward and Great Hall now house the Museum of Somerset. Particular treasures of the museum are the Shapwick canoe, an Iron Age boat discovered in a peat bog near Glastonbury which is the sort of vessel that would have been a common sight on the rivers and wetlands of Somerset around 2,000 years ago, and a Roman mosaic floor found during excavations at Low Ham, west of Somerton; it depicts the story of Dido and Aeneas and is unique to Britain in that its five panels make up a story, making it one of the earliest examples of narrative art in the country. After the castle, the oldest building in Taunton is the old Tudor Tavern at number 15 Fore Street, the four-storey jettied building seen in the centre of this view. Its frontage dates from 1578, but the rest of the building is probably 14th-century. It currently (2012) houses a branch of Caffè Nero.

In June 1685 the Duke of Monmouth arrived in Taunton at the start of his doomed attempt to topple his uncle King James II and take the throne. He was proclaimed King James III in Taunton's market place, and a group of young Taunton schoolgirls presented him with a banner they had embroidered. After the Monmouth rebellion failed, the 'Maids of Taunton' were arrested and imprisoned as part of the savage retribution that was meted out to the West Country. Several of them were under ten years old, and when they were brought before Judge Jeffreys, he raved at one so savagely that she collapsed and died of fear a few hours later. The rest of the Maids were cast into prison, where one of them died of fever, and King James II's queen and her maids of honour were granted the right to charge a heavy ransom from their relatives for their release.

One of the most beautiful church towers in Somerset is that of the Church of St Mary Magdalene in Taunton, approached off Hammet Street (seen in the photograph on page 49 of this book). The tower is 50 metres (163 feet) high and is built of Old Red Quantock sandstone and Ham Hill stone in Perpendicular Gothic design. It was described by Simon Jenkins in 'England's Thousand Best Churches' (2000) as 'the finest in England. It makes its peace with the sky not just with a coronet but with the entire crown jewels cast in red-brown stone'. What we see today is a rebuild that was completed in 1862, to the lines of the original 15th-century design. During the rebuild of the tower a donkey powered the pulley which took the stone up to the workmen. When the work was completed, the donkey was taken up to the top of the tower to see the result of its labours and admire the view! Beside the church is Whirligig Lane – this got its unusual name because in late medieval times the lane led to a narrow gateway through the town defences that was just wide enough for pedestrians, where there was a turnstile or whirligig through which people could pass.

5 miles north-west of Taunton is Bishops Lydeard, which is the southern terminus of the West Somerset Railway. This is the longest preserved steam heritage railway line in the country, running for 22.75 miles along a beautifully scenic route from Bishops Lydeard to its northern terminus at Minehead. At just under 120 metres (400 feet) above sea level the highest station on the line is at Crowcombe Heathfield, 2 miles west of the village of Crowcombe, which has been used as a period station location in several films and TV series, including the 1964 Beatles' film 'A Hard Day's Night'.

Both Bishops Lydeard and Crowcombe are famous for the medieval carved wooden bench ends in their churches. Those at St Mary's Church at Bishops Lydeard feature a windmill, a medieval sailing ship and a pelican feeding her chicks with blood pecked from her breast, an image used in medieval religious art as an allegorical depiction of Jesus in his sacrificial love. The church at Bishops Lydeard is also renowned for its spectacular 16th-century rood screen, with beautifully carved panels. Crowcombe's fine parish church of the Holy Ghost features a series of bench ends carved with images of some very strange Green Men, including one with mermen coming out of his ears, as well as a panel showing men fighting a two-headed winged lizard or dragon, possibly depicting the 'Gurt Vurm' of nearby Shervage Wood of local legend.

About ten miles south-west of Taunton is Wellington. In 1814 Arthur Wellesley (1769-1852) was granted the estate of the town when he was elevated to the peerage in thanks for his military successes, first in India and then in the Iberian Peninsula against Napoleon's armies; he adopted its name for his title, becoming the 1st Duke of Wellington. He subsequently commanded the allied forces in their victory against Napoleon at the Battle of Waterloo in 1815. A commemorative monument to the Duke stands on Wellington Hill to the south of the town, erected to celebrate his victory at Waterloo. Its tall pointed design was inspired by an Egyptian obelisk, but is in the shape of the bayonet used by the soldiers of the Duke's armies.

Another famous soldier in British military history is commemorated at Hatch Beauchamp, off the A358 between Taunton and Ilminster. The south chancel window in its parish church is dedicated to Colonel John Rouse Merriott Chard, VC, RE (1847-1897) who died in the village and was buried in the churchyard; his brother the Reverend C E Chard was the Rector of Hatch Beauchamp from 1885 until 1911. In 1879, as a Lieutenant in the Royal Engineers, Colonel Chard had been the commanding officer at the defence of the mission station of Rorke's Drift in the Anglo-Zulu War in South Africa, when around 150 British and colonial troops successfully held out against a sustained attack by 3,000-4,000 Zulu warriors, for which he won the Victoria Cross – he was immortalised in the popular feature film about the engagement, 'Zulu', of 1964, in which he was played by the actor Stanley Baker.

The name of Ilminster means 'the minster, or church, near the River Isle', a reference to the town's large church of St Mary. The church is renowned for its superb, lavishly decorated west tower and impressive tie beam roof, both of which date from its rebuilding in the 15th century. Much of the work was financed by Sir William Wadham, who died in 1452 and whose ornate table tomb is in the Wadham Chapel of the church, adorned with a fine memorial brass of Sir William and his mother Joan – a brass commemorating a mother and son is a most unusual combination. Sir William Wadham is represented wearing a complete suit of plate armour exported to England from Milanese armourers; this was the finest armour of the period, its most distinctive features being the heavy reinforcements to the left shoulder and elbow, and long, pointed gauntlet cuffs. Sir William's mother Lady Joan is depicted wearing an ungirdled kirtle and long mantle, her head covered with a wimple with a pleated barbe beneath her chin.

CHARD, FORE STREET 1907 58761

A sleepy Somerset market town might not seem the obvious birthplace of powered flight, but that is what Chard in South Somerset can claim to be. In the 1820s John Stringfellow (1799-1883) came to work in Chard, originally making bobbins and carriages for the town's lace-making industry, which was becoming increasingly mechanised at that time, but later working on steam engines. Also working in Chard's lace-making industry was William Samuel Henson (1812-1888). Both men were interested in the possibility of powered flight, and in the early 1840s they collaborated on designs for an 'Aerial Steam Carriage', but without success. Henson then became discouraged and eventually emigrated to America, but John Stringfellow continued to work on his ideas and in 1848 he achieved the first powered flight with a small steam-driven flying machine, when it flew for a distance of nearly 37 metres (120 feet) in a disused lace factory in Chard. Stringfellow's original flying machine, 3 metres (10 feet) long, is now on display in the Science Museum in London, but a bronze model of that first primitive aircraft can be seen in Fore Street in Chard, a short distance from the Guildhall.

Seven miles east of Chard is Crewkerne, a market town that became wealthy in the Middle Ages through the wool and cloth trade. In the 18th and 19th centuries the town's prosperity derived from a flourishing flax industry, which employed almost a quarter of the population and produced sailcloth for the Royal Navy until steam supplanted sail. Crewkerne's superb Perpendicular-style parish church of St Bartholomew was largely built from the wool wealth of the medieval town, and is one of the finest 15th-century churches in the county. On one side its huge windows leave room for little more than buttresses between, and its monumental west front is like that of Bath Abbey. The exterior of the church is decorated with gargoyles, and amongst many other notable features of the church are some rather quaint stone carvings in the south porch of musicians playing medieval instruments, and two rather fearsome 'Green Man' carvings inside the building.

Other notable churches in this part of Somerset are the Church of St Peter and St Paul at South Petherton, whose Early English octagonal tower culminating in a short spire is said to be the highest of its type in the country, and the Church of All Saints at Martock, where the magnificent carved oak angel roof of the nave interior, dating from the early 16th century, is one of the finest examples of woodwork in a Somerset church. The roof is made up of six bays in a so-called 'quilted' arrangement, with each bay containing 128 individually carved panels, whilst the carved tie beams support carved wooden angels.

Angels of a rather different kind can be seen inside the Church of St Peter and St Paul at Muchelney, about four miles north-west of Martock. The panels of the wagon ceiling of this church are spectacularly decorated with brightly coloured paintings of clouds, cherubs and rather camp-looking angels in various states of dress and undress, some of which are bare-breasted; they are often described as the 'topless angels' or the 'naughty angels'. They were painted in the early 17th century, and it has been suggested that their nudity was supposed to symbolise their innocent purity.

One of the most beautiful country houses in Somerset is Montacute House, a few miles west of Yeovil. This superb E-plan Elizabethan country house of the 1590s is now in the care of the National Trust, and its top-storey long gallery contains the Tudor collections of the National Portrait Gallery. A famous feature of the house is a long plaster frieze in the hall, dating from the early 17th century, that depicts a rustic scene of a 'skimmington', a way that people of a local community in the past ritually humiliated a member of a married couple, perhaps because one of them was an adulterer, or because the man was a wife-beater or because, as here, they wanted to mock a hen-pecked husband. The skimmington frieze in Montacute House tells the story of a husband whose wife catches him having a drink whilst minding the baby and hits him over the head with a shoe. This is witnessed by a neighbour, and a group of villages then parade the man around the village astride a pole, whilst he is made to play a flute.

MONTACUTE, MONTACUTE HOUSE 1900 45500

YEOVIL, MIDDLE STREET 1903   49166

Yeovil has been extensively redeveloped since the mid 20th century and this part of lower Middle Street looks very different now from this view of 1903 – all the buildings have disappeared, and the left-hand side is a pedestrian precinct called Glovers Walk in memory of the glove-making that was Yeovil's major industry from the 13th to the 20th centuries. An older building of the town that still survives further up Middle Street now houses the Yeovil branch of WH Smith, but was formerly the town's Post Office. If you look high up on its corner with Union Street you can see reminders of that previous role in the two small stone squirrels perched on the frontage above the three-bay window on the upper storey, representing the Post Office Savings Bank.

The beautiful church of St John the Baptist in the town centre is Yeovil's oldest surviving building. Two stained glass windows of the church are unique in English churches because the scenes depicted in them show the disciple Judas with a black halo, representing his treachery to Jesus. One appears in the Garden of Gethsemane in the eastern window above the high altar, while the other can be found in the Last Supper in the window in the south transept.

North of Yeovil on the A303 is Sparkford, home of the famous Haynes International Motor Museum. There are over 400 vintage, veteran and classic cars, motorcycles and speedway bikes in its collection, including historic vehicles dating from the very early years of motoring, nostalgic classics from the 1950s and 60s and exciting super cars of modern times. A particular feature is Hall 2, known as 'The Red Room', which displays 50 sports cars of various eras from all around the world, all of which are bright red.

Moving westwards towards Wincanton, just south of the A303 is Compton Pauncefoot, a village whose name has rather delightfully recorded for posterity the nickname of a Norman knight who held the manor at some time in the early Middle Ages – the 'compton' part of the name means 'a narrow valley', but the 'pauncefoot' part comes from the original version of 'pauncefote', meaning 'fat paunch', or 'fat belly'!

Wincanton in South Somerset is unique in Britain for being twinned with a town that can only be found in fiction. As well as having twin-town status with Gennes and Les Rosiers-sur-Loire in France and Lahnau in Germany, in 2002 Wincanton was twinned with Ankh-Morpork, a fictional city-state created by the author Terry Pratchett in his 'Discworld' series of fantasy novels. The twinning scheme was the idea of Bernard Pearson who runs a shop in Wincanton called The Cunning Artificer which deals in Discworld memorabilia and now doubles as the Ankh-Morpork consulate. In 2009 a number of roads in the Kingwell Rise area of Wincanton were named after places in the Discworld books, such as Peach Pie Street and Treacle Mine Road, after local residents were asked to vote on a shortlist of 14 names suggested by Terry Pratchett, who lived in Somerset for many years. The author visited the town on the 5th of April 2009 to unveil the road names and commented on the scheme: 'I think it's a lovely idea, even though it makes my head spin to think of the books becoming a little closer to reality.'

CASTLE CARY, THE TOWN HALL AND ROUND HOUSE c1960 C61106lx

North-west of Wincanton is Castle Cary. As its name suggests, there was once a castle there, on Lodge Hill overlooking the town, but only its earthworks now remain. The arcaded building seen in this view was the Market Hall. Originally erected in 1616, it was rebuilt in 1855 and now serves as the town's information centre and museum. The small domed building in the background of this view is the old Round House on Bailey Hill, the town's tiny prison which was built in 1779. In 1785 a resolution was passed that all children over seven who did not attend the town's Sunday School and were caught playing were to be locked up there. Hopefully not too many unfortunate children were incarcerated there on a Sunday, since the building is only 2.1 metres (7 feet) in diameter, and some of that space is taken up by a stone privy! These old lock-ups, often known as 'blind houses', were once a common feature in England's towns and villages, but only a few still survive; there is another good example in Somerset at Pensford, west of Bath.

SPORTING SOMERSET

The headquarters of Somerset County Cricket Club, founded in 1875, lie on the south bank of the River Tone in Taunton. In 1946 M M Walford scored 100 in his first match for the county against India, becoming the first player to do so at Taunton. Over the years the county ground has seen many fine players and teams, including of course the great Somerset side of the 1970s which included Ian Botham, Viv Richards and Joel Garner. Famous players in the club's history are recalled in the names of the Colin Atkinson Pavilion, the Sir Ian Botham Stand, the Marcus Trescothick Stand and the Andy Caddick Pavilion. The county ground at Taunton has also been the headquarters of the England Women's Cricket Team since 2006.

Founded in 1865, Bath Rugby Football Club is one of the oldest and most successful rugby union clubs in the country. It is a tradition that whenever Bath RFC play Llanelli RFC a rag doll is hung on one of the uprights of the cross bar to 'watch' the game. Afterwards, the doll is dressed in the colours of the winning team and given to that team to keep until the next encounter.

Set into the pavement in front of the shops in the Market Place in Wells is a long thin brass plaque decorated with the symbol of the five Olympic rings that commemorates one of Britain's sporting heroines, Mary Rand, née Bignal, who was born in Wells in 1940 and grew up there, winning an athletics scholarship to Millfield School at nearby Street. The simple brass strip marks the distance of 6.76m (22ft 2¼ inches) covered by Mary Rand when she created the world record in the ladies' long-jump event at the Tokyo Olympic Games in 1964 and became the first-ever British female athlete to win a track and field Olympic Gold medal. She also won both a Silver and a Bronze medal in the same Games – Silver in the pentathlon event and Bronze as part of the Great Britain team that finished third in the 4 x 100 metres relay.

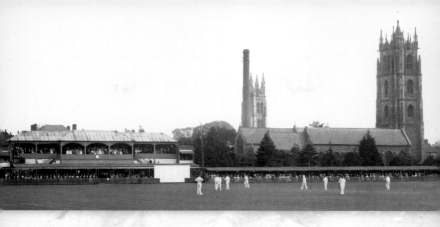

TAUNTON, THE COUNTY CRICKET GROUND 1902 48716

Somerset gained its first Football League club at the end of the 2002/03 season, when Yeovil Town FC won the Conference League championship by a record 17 points and were promoted to Division Three. Nicknamed The Glovers after Yeovil's glove-making industry of the past, the club won the League Two championship at the end of 2004/5 season, winning promotion to League One where they currently play (2012).

Weston-super-Mare stages a motocross event called the Weston Beach Race every autumn, which is one of the most famous beach races in the country. The event has been held since 1983 and also features races for junior riders, sidecarcross riders and quad bikers. Over 1,000 riders descend on the town to race on the wide sands of Weston's beach, and crowds of up to 100,000 people flock to the resort to watch the event.

A famous son of Frome is the Formula One racing driver Jenson Button, who won the Formula One World Championship in 2009. He was born in the town in 1980 and brought up in the area, attending Vallis First School, Selwood Middle School and Frome Community College. Jenson Avenue in the town has been named after him, as has the Jenson Button Bridge over the River Frome that runs through the town.

QUIZ QUESTIONS

Answers on page 52.

1. In Somerset dialect, what is a 'dumbledore'?

2. Whereabouts in Somerset can you find what legend says is a wedding party turned to stone?

3. Which well-known chain of shoe shops started in Somerset?

4. Whereabouts in Somerset can you find 'The Willow Man', and what is it?

5. What are 'hunky punks'?

6. If you come from Somerset and like your beer, you have probably discovered one of the county's most famous drinking holes, popularly known as Eli's. Where is it, what is its proper name, and what is so special about it?

7. Somerset has more 'Thankful Villages' than any other county in the UK. What are these?

8. 2 miles north of Langport in central Somerset is Stembridge Tower Mill, built in 1822 and now in the care of the National Trust. What is special about this windmill?

9. What is the connection between Somerset and the nursery rhyme about Jack and Jill who went up the hill to fetch a pail of water?

10. Whereabouts in Somerset can you climb Jacob's Ladder?

TAUNTON
THE CHURCH OF
ST MARY MAGDALENE
1888 20859

RECIPE

SOMERSET CHEESE BAKE

Cheddar is a small town in Somerset which has given its name to a cheese that has now become world famous. Originally, the cheese had to be produced within 30 miles of Wells Cathedral to be classed as 'Cheddar cheese'. The type of cheese made by the 'cheddaring' process has become so popular that is now made all over the world and the name 'Cheddar cheese' has no Protected Designation of Origin (PDO) within the European Union, but only Cheddar produced from local milk within four counties of south-west England – Somerset, Dorset, Devon and Cornwall – may use the name 'West Country Farmhouse Cheddar'.

> 350g/12oz Cheddar cheese, grated
> 3 onions, peeled and very finely sliced
> Salt and pepper
> 175g/6oz fresh breadcrumbs, preferably wholemeal
> 6 tablespoonfuls of milk
> 25g/1oz butter

Pre-heat the oven to 180°C/350°F/Gas Mark 4. Grease a shallow ovenproof dish.

Reserve a little of the cheese and breadcrumbs to use as a topping for the pudding, then use the rest to put a layer of cheese, then a layer of onion, and then a layer of breadcrumbs in the dish., seasoning each layer to taste with salt and pepper. Pour on the milk, and finish with a layer of most of the remaining cheese, then all the reserved breadcrumbs, and sprinkle the top with the rest of the cheese. Dot the top with small pieces of butter. Bake in the pre-heated oven for 35-40 minutes, until the onion is cooked and the top is crisp and brown.

RECIPE

CIDER CAKE

Think of Somerset, and most people associate this area with cider. The secret of making good cider is the skilled blending of juice from several varieties of cider apples, many of which have delightful names such as Slack-ma-girdle and Poor Man's Profit.

> 225g/8oz mixed sultanas, raisins and currants
> 150ml/5 fl oz/ ¼ pint cider
> 175g/6oz butter or margarine, softened to room temperature
> 175g/6oz soft brown sugar
> 3 eggs, beaten
> 225g/8oz self-raising flour
>   (either white or wholemeal SR flour works well)
> 1 teaspoonful mixed spice

Soak the dried fruit in the cider overnight, or at least 12 hours before making the cake.

Pre-heat the oven to 180°C/350°F/Gas Mark 4. Grease a 20-24cms (8-9 inches) round or square cake tin and line it with greaseproof paper. Cream the butter or margarine, add the sugar and cream until light and fluffy. Lightly beat the eggs and gradually beat them into the mixture, a little at a time, adding a spoonful of flour to prevent curdling. Stir in the soaked dried fruit and remaining cider. Add the flour and mixed spice, mix thoroughly and beat well. Pour the mixture into the prepared tin and bake just below the centre of the pre-heated oven for about 1 hour and 10 minutes, until the surface is risen and firm to the touch, and a skewer inserted into the middle comes out clean – cover the top with a piece of kitchen foil or greaseproof paper if it seems to be browning too quickly. Leave to settle in the tin for 5 minutes, then turn out onto a wire rack to cool completely.

QUIZ ANSWERS

1. 'Dumbledore' is a Somerset dialect word for a bumble bee.

2. At Stanton Drew in north-east Somerset, where there are three prehistoric stone circles. According to folklore, the stones of the circles are members of a wedding party that was held here in the past. The revellers let their celebrations go on past midnight and spill over into Sunday, and were turned into stone by the Devil for dancing on the Sabbath.

3. Clarks, which was founded in Street in 1825 by the brothers Cyrus and James Clark. The business began when James Clark was working at a tannery owned by Cyrus and had the idea of using up offcuts of sheepskin and leather to make slippers. The company expanded into making shoes, and became a major employer in Street. The production of Clarks shoes was moved abroad in the 1990s but the company's headquarters is still in Street, where it also houses a museum about shoemaking. Street's shoemaking heritage is also recalled in the name of the Crispin Hall, which was donated to the town by Clarks and named after St Crispin, the patron saint of shoemakers.

4. Willow-growing and basket making have been traditional industries of the Somerset Levels for centuries, and are commemorated with a huge woven-willow sculpture called the 'The Willow Man' that stands beside the M5 outside Bridgwater. The structure was the work of willow artist Serena de la Hey. At 12 metres (40 feet) tall, it is the largest willow figure in the UK, and probably in the world.

5. 'Hunky punks' is the Somerset dialect name for the grotesque figures carved from stone that decorate many of the county's churches and are similar to gargoyles. The difference is that hunky punks have a purely ornamental purpose, whereas gargoyles are actually decorative water spouts, discharging water from the roof through their mouths.

6. Eli's is the popular name for the Rose and Crown pub at Huish Episcopi, near Langport. It is known as Eli's after Elijah Scott, a previous landlord. The old-fashioned interior of the pub is like going back in time – there is no bar, but a flagstone-floored taproom where beer and cider is served straight from the barrels.

7. Thankful Villages was the term used for villages where all the local men who went off to fight in the First World War returned alive when the war was over. Somerset has the highest number of Thankful Villages in the UK, but even so there were only 9 places in the county where no men were killed in that dreadful conflict: Aisholt, Chantry, Chelwood, Priddy, Rodney Stoke, Stanton Prior, Stocklinch, Tellisford and Woolley. The sad lists of names inscribed on war memorials in other villages and towns around the county commemorate the men who didn't come home.

8. Stembridge Tower Mill is the last remaining thatched windmill in England, and the only survivor of five thatched mills that once stood in the area.

9. Kilmersdon, south of Radstock, is linked to the nursery rhyme 'Jack and Jill'. They are believed to have been a couple living in the village in the 16th century who every day went up the hillside behind the old toll-house for water from the well next to Kilmersdon Primary School. The footpath they used, leading up the hill from Ames Lane to the school, was a dangerous route often strewn with rocks, and it appears that Jack was killed by a rock fall. Both the footpath and the well-head in the school grounds were restored in 1999 as part of a Millennium project. There are now stones markers along the route, each of which depicts a line from the nursery rhyme.

10. At Cheddar. Jacob's Ladder is a series of 274 steps that leads up the side of Cheddar Gorge to an observational tower.

FRANCIS FRITH

PIONEER   VICTORIAN   PHOTOGRAPHER

Francis Frith, founder of the world-famous photographic archive, was a complex and multi-talented man. A devout Quaker and a highly successful Victorian businessman, he was philosophical by nature and pioneering in outlook. By 1855 he had already established a wholesale grocery business in Liverpool, and sold it for the astonishing sum of £200,000, which is the equivalent today of over £15,000,000. Now in his thirties, and captivated by the new science of photography, Frith set out on a series of pioneering journeys up the Nile and to the Near East.

INTRIGUE AND EXPLORATION

He was the first photographer to venture beyond the sixth cataract of the Nile. Africa was still the mysterious 'Dark Continent', and Stanley and Livingstone's historic meeting was a decade into the future. The conditions for picture taking confound belief. He laboured for hours in his wicker dark-room in the sweltering heat of the desert, while the volatile chemicals fizzed dangerously in their trays. Back in London he exhibited his photographs and was 'rapturously cheered' by members of the Royal Society. His reputation as a photographer was made overnight.

VENTURE OF A LIFE-TIME

By the 1870s the railways had threaded their way across the country, and Bank Holidays and half-day Saturdays had been made obligatory by Act of Parliament. All of a sudden the working man and his family were able to enjoy days out, take holidays, and see a little more of the world.

With typical business acumen, Francis Frith foresaw that these new tourists would enjoy having souvenirs to commemorate their days out. For the next thirty years he travelled the country by train and by pony and trap, producing fine photographs of seaside resorts and beauty spots that were keenly bought by millions of Victorians. These prints were painstakingly pasted into family albums and pored over during the dark nights of winter, rekindling precious memories of summer excursions. Frith's studio was soon supplying retail shops all over the country, and by 1890 F Frith & Co had become the greatest specialist photographic publishing company in the world, with over 2,000 sales outlets, and pioneered the picture postcard.

FRANCIS FRITH'S LEGACY

Francis Frith had died in 1898 at his villa in Cannes, his great project still growing. By 1970 the archive he created contained over a third of a million pictures showing 7,000 British towns and villages.

Frith's legacy to us today is of immense significance and value, for the magnificent archive of evocative photographs he created provides a unique record of change in the cities, towns and villages throughout Britain over a century and more. Frith and his fellow studio photographers revisited locations many times down the years to update their views, compiling for us an enthralling and colourful pageant of British life and character.

We are fortunate that Frith was dedicated to recording the minutiae of everyday life. For it is this sheer wealth of visual data, the painstaking chronicle of changes in dress, transport, street layouts, buildings, housing and landscape that captivates us so much today, offering us a powerful link with the past and with the lives of our ancestors.

Computers have now made it possible for Frith's many thousands of images to be accessed almost instantly. The archive offers every one of us an opportunity to examine the places where we and our families have lived and worked down the years. Its images, depicting our shared past, are now bringing pleasure and enlightenment to millions around the world a century and more after his death.

For further information visit: www.francisfrith.com

INTERIOR DECORATION

Frith's photographs can be seen framed and as giant wall murals in thousands of pubs, restaurants, hotels, banks, retail stores and other public buildings throughout Britain. These provide interesting and attractive décor, generating strong local interest and acting as a powerful reminder of gentler days in our increasingly busy and frenetic world.

FRITH PRODUCTS

All Frith photographs are available as prints and posters in a variety of different sizes and styles. In the UK we also offer a range of other gift and stationery products illustrated with Frith photographs, although many of these are not available for delivery outside the UK – see our web site for more information on the products available for delivery in your country.

THE INTERNET

Over 100,000 photographs of Britain can be viewed and purchased on the Frith web site. The web site also includes memories and reminiscences contributed by our customers, who have personal knowledge of localities and of the people and properties depicted in Frith photographs. If you wish to learn more about a specific town or village you may find these reminiscences fascinating to browse. Why not add your own comments if you think they would be of interest to others? See **www.francisfrith.com**

PLEASE HELP US BRING FRITH'S PHOTOGRAPHS TO LIFE

Our authors do their best to recount the history of the places they write about. They give insights into how particular towns and villages developed, they describe the architecture of streets and buildings, and they discuss the lives of famous people who lived there. But however knowledgeable our authors are, the story they tell is necessarily incomplete.

Frith's photographs are so much more than plain historical documents. They are living proofs of the flow of human life down the generations. They show real people at real moments in history; and each of those people is the son or daughter of someone, the brother or sister, aunt or uncle, grandfather or grandmother of someone else. All of them lived, worked and played in the streets depicted in Frith's photographs.

We would be grateful if you would give us your insights into the places shown in our photographs: the streets and buildings, the shops, businesses and industries. Post your memories of life in those streets on the Frith website: what it was like growing up there, who ran the local shop and what shopping was like years ago; if your workplace is shown tell us about your working day and what the building is used for now. Read other visitors' memories and reconnect with your shared local history and heritage. With your help more and more Frith photographs can be brought to life, and vital memories preserved for posterity, and for the benefit of historians in the future.

Wherever possible, we will try to include some of your comments in future editions of our books. Moreover, if you spot errors in dates, titles or other facts, please let us know, because our archive records are not always completely accurate—they rely on 140 years of human endeavour and hand-compiled records. You can email us using the contact form on the website.

Thank you!

For further information, trade, or author enquiries
please contact us at the address below:

**The Francis Frith Collection, Oakley Business Park,
Wylye Road, Dinton, Wiltshire SP3 5EU.**
Tel: +44 (0)1722 716 376 Fax: +44 (0)1722 716 881
e-mail: sales@francisfrith.co.uk **www.francisfrith.com**